UNITED

£7.99

A Pillar Box Red Publication

we ♥ love you...

THE WANTED

An Unauthorised 2012 Annual

Written by Sarah Delmege
Designed by Chris Dalrymple

Contents

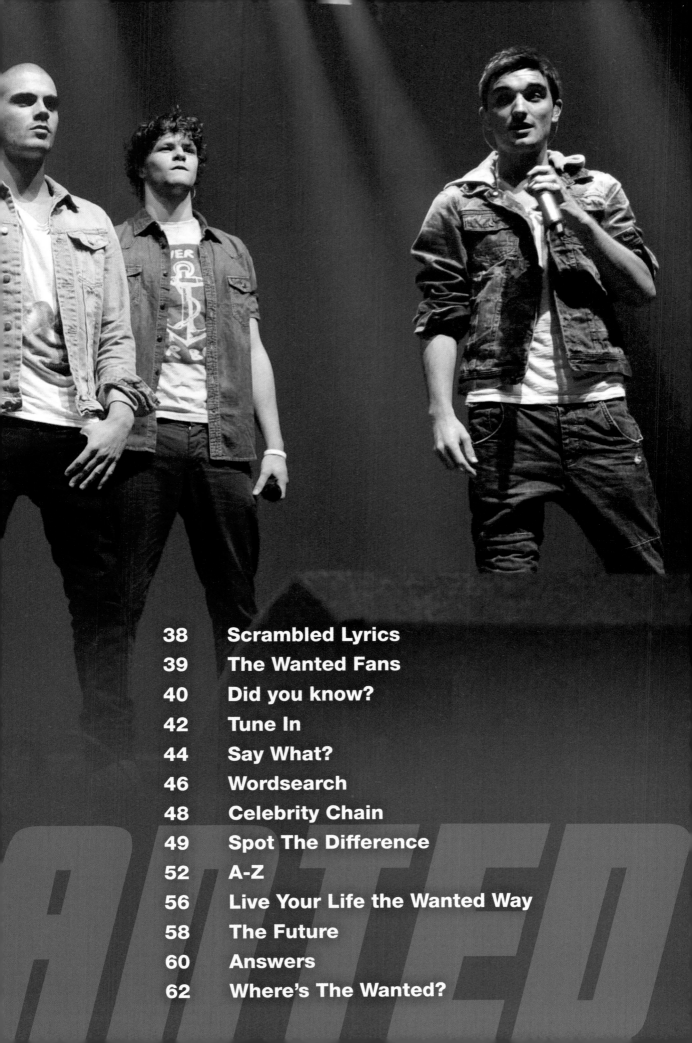

we ♥ love you...
THE WANTED
Because...

You don't let your success go to your heads.

You're ordinary lads who are up for a laugh.

You're all mega-talented.

Your music is different to any other boy band out there.

You write loads of your own songs.

You've developed your own sense of style and always look great.

You all really like each other and get on amazingly well.

You love your fans and know you wouldn't be where you are without them!

NATHAN

Name: Nathan James Sykes

Hometown: Gloucester

Date of birth: 18 April 1993

Star sign: Aries

Height: 5'9"

Hair: brown

Favourite food: spag bol, Chinese, soup, roast dinners.

Favourite band: Boyz II Men

Football team: Manchester United

Favourite animal: cat

Favourite TV show: Match of the Day, Britain's Got Talent

Role in band: The baby

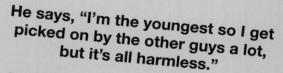

He says, "I'm the youngest so I get picked on by the other guys a lot, but it's all harmless."

Before the band: "Studying. I took my drama exams."

Ideal girl: "I'm not too fussy, but I do prefer quiet girls."

Did you know? "I kissed Britney Spears when I was 10 and performing on Saturday morning TV. All my friends were so jealous."

JAMES

Name: James McGuiness

Hometown: Nottingham

Date of birth: 24 July 1990

Star sign: Leo

Height: 6'1"

Eyes: blue

Hair: brown

Favourite food: pizza, pasta with pesto, chips, cheese toasties, Starbars, eggs in any form

Favourite bands: Coldplay, Newton Faulkner, Florence, Jack Penate, Damien Rice

Football team: Celtic

Favourite animal: chimp

Favourite TV show: anything with David Attenborough, Misfits

Role in band: The joker

He says, "I'm the goofy one of the group. I'm always mucking about and you can count on me being in a good mood through to the end of the day."

Before the band: "I was a waiter part-time and studying."

Ideal girl: "I don't like girls who are up themselves. I'm a goofball and I'll often say something silly to a hot girl, and they'll just look at me disgusted!"

Did you know? "I seriously hate polystyrene – it makes me feel sick."

SIVA

Name: Siva Kaneswaran

Hometown: Dublin

Date of birth: 16 November 1988

Star sign: Scorpio

Height: 6'1"

Eyes: brown

Hair: black

Favourite food: stew, brownies, shepherd's pie.

Favourite band: Switchfoot

Football team: Manchester City or Bolton

Favourite animal: dog

Favourite TV show: Family Guy

Role in band: The self-confessed hottie

He says, "Tall, dark and handsome and Zen. I'm the mellow one in the band."

Before the band: "I modeled at Storm for a year and a half, but was really just desperate to get back into music – so here I am."

Ideal girl: "A good cook and someone good humoured. I don't have a certain type – if you could have it you have it. It could be you, it could be anyone."

Did you know: "I switch off a lot and forget where I am."

TOM

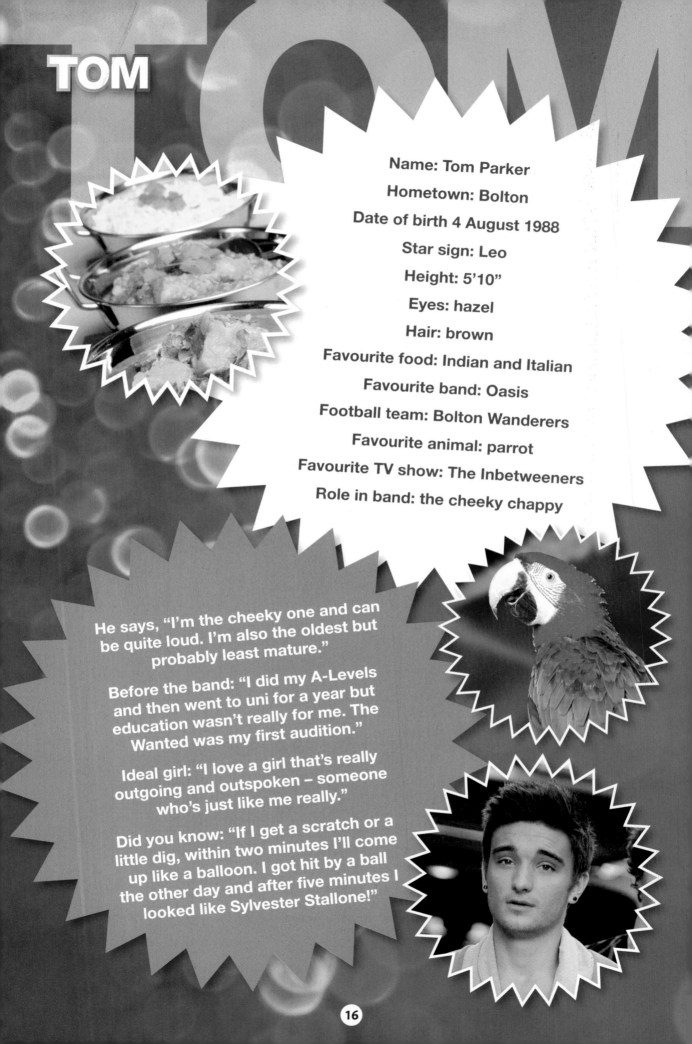

Name: Tom Parker

Hometown: Bolton

Date of birth 4 August 1988

Star sign: Leo

Height: 5'10"

Eyes: hazel

Hair: brown

Favourite food: Indian and Italian

Favourite band: Oasis

Football team: Bolton Wanderers

Favourite animal: parrot

Favourite TV show: The Inbetweeners

Role in band: the cheeky chappy

He says, "I'm the cheeky one and can be quite loud. I'm also the oldest but probably least mature."

Before the band: "I did my A-Levels and then went to uni for a year but education wasn't really for me. The Wanted was my first audition."

Ideal girl: "I love a girl that's really outgoing and outspoken – someone who's just like me really."

Did you know: "If I get a scratch or a little dig, within two minutes I'll come up like a balloon. I got hit by a ball the other day and after five minutes I looked like Sylvester Stallone!"

MAX

Name: Maximillian Alberto George

Hometown: Manchester

Date of birth: 6 September 1988

Star sign: Virgo

Height: 5'8"

Eyes: grey

Hair: dark brown

Favourite food: Dominos pizza, full English breakfast, rare steak

Favourite band: Queen

Football team: Manchester city

Favourite animal: Great white shark

Favourite TV show: The X Factor

Role in band: The Charmer

He says, "I'm the most experienced one being in a band before – the daddy of the group."

Before the band: "I was in Avenue for three and a half years, and before that I played football for Manchester City and Bolton."

Ideal girl: "I'm into girls that aren't bothered by money and going to flash places."

Did you know: "I like playing with people's ears. It's a comfort thing."

18

HOW IT ALL BEGAN

The Wanted story began in 2009 when Maximum Artist Management – who also look after The Saturdays – placed an advert in The Stage magazine, looking for members for a boy band.

Hundreds of wannabe pop stars turned up, ready to strut their stuff. Maximum Artist Management watched each of them closely. How did they project themselves? Did they have that mysterious and elusive star quality? Songs could be bought, routines could be choreographed, but a guy either had charisma, something that set him apart, or he didn't. It's not something you can fake, force or buy.

It was an intense and demanding process – but it was worth the wait. Nine long, gruelling months later, Maximum Artist Management were in no doubt – they had their band. Step forward Tom, Max, Jay, Siva and Nathan. Five very different lads – in personality, age, height and interests, who together equalled something magical.

The boys liked each other from the start. "We're all different characters and we all get on so well," says Tom. They all know how to have a good laugh, but they are professionals at heart and hungry for success.

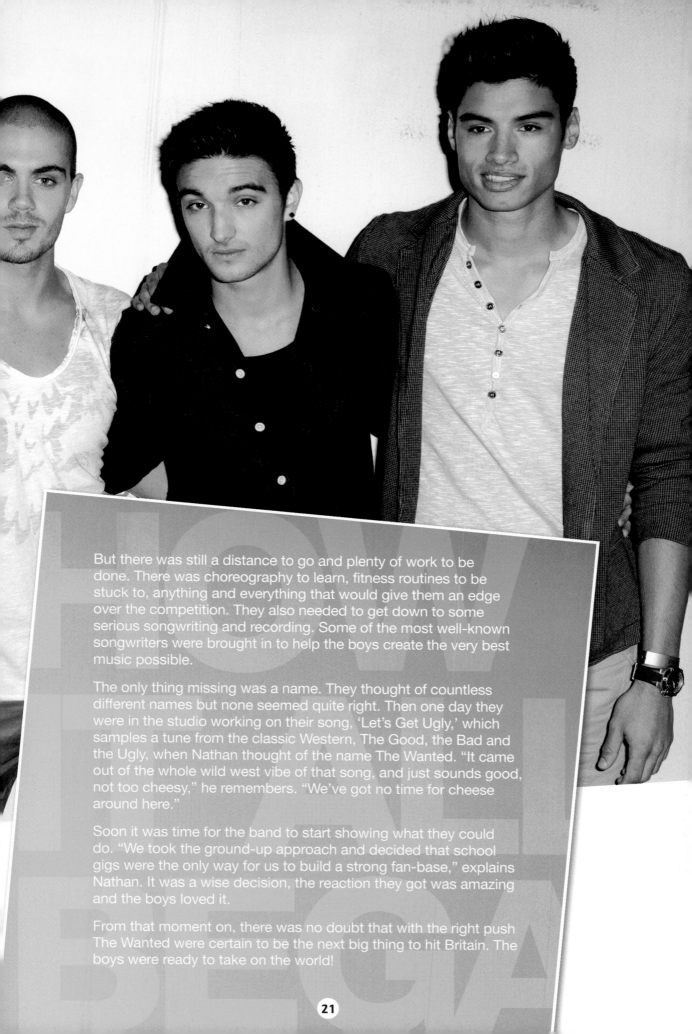

But there was still a distance to go and plenty of work to be done. There was choreography to learn, fitness routines to be stuck to, anything and everything that would give them an edge over the competition. They also needed to get down to some serious songwriting and recording. Some of the most well-known songwriters were brought in to help the boys create the very best music possible.

The only thing missing was a name. They thought of countless different names but none seemed quite right. Then one day they were in the studio working on their song, 'Let's Get Ugly,' which samples a tune from the classic Western, The Good, the Bad and the Ugly, when Nathan thought of the name The Wanted. "It came out of the whole wild west vibe of that song, and just sounds good, not too cheesy," he remembers. "We've got no time for cheese around here."

Soon it was time for the band to start showing what they could do. "We took the ground-up approach and decided that school gigs were the only way for us to build a strong fan-base," explains Nathan. It was a wise decision, the reaction they got was amazing and the boys loved it.

From that moment on, there was no doubt that with the right push The Wanted were certain to be the next big thing to hit Britain. The boys were ready to take on the world!

THINGS YOU DIDN'T KNOW

Max has four lizards back home.

The lads reckon Nathan is the shyest one around girls.

The way to win Siva over is to cook him something special.

Max hates dry sponges!

Siva's trousers once fell down while performing on stage!

The lads wrote approximately 50% of the songs on their first album.

Siva has an identical twin brother who's signed to a top modeling agency where Siva used to work too.

Tom plays the guitar and piano.

Max's dad once gave some stranded fans the money to get a taxi home from a concert.

Their bachelor pad in South London is so messy that two cleaners have quit already!

They are liked by over 100,000 people on Facebook.

Nathan plays the bagpipes!

Avenue (Max's old band) were disqualified from the X Factor because they already had a management deal.

ARE YOU *THE WANTED'S* BIGGEST FAN?

Take our mega quiz and find out!

MEGA QUIZ

1. Which member of The Wanted was once kissed by Britney Spears?
- a) Max
- b) Nathan
- c) Jay

MEGA QUIZ

2. Which band member is NOT a huge footie fan?
- a) Siva
- b) Max
- c) Jay

MEGA QUIZ

3. Who's favourite kids TV show is Teenage Mutant Ninja Turtles
- a) Tom
- b) Max
- c) Nathan

MEGA QUIZ

4. Who does not have a twin brother?
- a) Siva
- b) Jay
- c) Max

5. Which star sign is Siva?

a) Scorpio

b) Capricorn

c) Aries

MEGA QUIZ

6. Which song does Max wish he'd written?

a) Wonderwall by Oasis

b) Angels by Robbie Williams

c) Sitting on the Dock Of The Bay by Otis Redding

MEGA QUIZ

7. Which of the lads went to The Sylvia Young Theatre School?

a) Jay

b) Nathan

c) Tom

MEGA QUIZ

8. Which film was the inspiration for The Wanted's name?

a) Grease

b) High School Musical

c) The Good, the Bad and the Ugly

MEGA QUIZ

9. What was Siva's occupation before he joined The Wanted

a) Model

b) Student

c) Professional footballer

MEGA QUIZ

10. Which band member hates fish?

a) Tom

b) Jay

c) Max

Answers on Page 60.

WHO'S YOUR MOST WANTED ?

Take a good look at this page – and choose your The Wanted crush.

Nathan is the shy one.

The girl he's looking for is: Faithful, focused and friendly but not too forward. Nathan is scared off by girls who are too noisy. You have been warned!

You can grab him by: Becoming his friend first.

So you should be: Loyal! When Nathan dates a girl he only has eyes for her, so he'll be looking for someone who'll show the same level of commitment. Don't be afraid to say how you feel, he loves a girl who's totally open with him.

"I love it when a girl can give good banter. It's going to sound weird but I love the way you can't win with a girl. If you ever have an argument, you can't win."

Tom is the cheeky chappy.

The girl he is looking for is: A fun-loving party girl who isn't afraid to make the first move!

You can grab him by: Starting an interesting conversation – Tom is a total sucker for brains as well as beauty.

So you should be: Bold! To win Tom's heart, you'll need to take the lead. So give him all the positive signals to show you're interested. Eye contact and smiles are a good place to start.

"Since being in the band, I'm more aware that people might just be interested in you for the status so it makes you more careful about meeting girls."

Jay is the joker.

The girl he's looking for is: Laid-back and good for a laugh.

You can grab him by: Letting your barriers down and being totally open.

So you should be: Laid-back. He likes to do the running and will want you make you laugh. The best way to win his heart, is to make eye contact so he notices you, then laugh out loud at his jokes and don't forget to show you can laugh at yourself too!

"I like it when girls are a bit different but really confident and funny."

Siva is the hottie.

The girl he's looking for is: Romantic, good humoured and a good cook.

You can grab him by: Making a huge romantic gesture like cooking him dinner by candlelight.

So you should be: A super whiz in the kitchen. Cook him something special and you'll definitely win him over, especially if you serve it with a huge, big smile on your face.

"To me sexiness is being confident, witty and a good cook."

Max is the charmer.

The girl he is looking for is: Down to earth, and not bothered by fame!

You can grab him by: A huge big cheeky smile, and by looking happy and approachable.

So you should be: Confident enough to stand out from the crowd, and equally happy whether you're dressed up to the nines in a club or chilling out in trackies and trainers at home.

"It's great when you meet someone who's up for a laugh, doesn't take themselves too seriously and likes to party."

LOVE WANTED

We've all got our favourite member and it seems the ladies of celebville are no different! We don't blame 'em.

Kate Thornton

Nathan managed to grab a cheeky kiss from his dream woman, Kate Thornton, when they appeared on a show. "She just happened to turn her face at the wrong time and I was puckering up. It was one of the best moments of my life."

Hayley Williams

Jay has a crush on the lead singer of American alternative rock band Paramore. "She's a cracker. She's beautiful. I've only seen her on TV but she's got the perfect mouth."

Rihanna

Siva met Rihanna at a club and the pair shared a dance. The couple have been in touch by text.

Michelle Keegan

Max is currently loved up with gorgeous Coronation Street star, Michelle. "I just see her as Michelle and she sees me as Max," he says.

Leona Lewis

After her split with long-term boyfriend Lou Al-Chamaa, Leona and Max were spotted chatting and flirting at famous London club Whiskey Mist.

WANTED

STYLE FILE

Looking good is very important for The Wanted lads. Girls love their looks and guys admire their casual, accessible style. Each member rocks his own unique style. From combats to high tops, checked shirts to blazers, one thing's for sure, the boys always look the business!

MAX

Max is the rough and ready member of the group. With his no-nonsense cropped hair, his relaxed street style looks effortless and cool without looking like he's trying too hard. He's a big fan of fuss-free chest-baring vests and carrot leg jeans paired with Converse trainers.

NATHAN

With his butter-wouldn't-melt looks and super sharp style, Nathan is the clean-cut member of the group. But he always gives his classic look a twist with an assortment of jewellery and worn-in trainers that give his style an edge.

TOM

This lad certainly knows how to work his military/workman look. He rocks casually cool baggy trousers and battered boots which are always off-set by his spiky hair, earrings and his ever-present cheeky smile.

SIVA

Tall, dark and impossibly handsome, the model-turned-singer boasts an impressive dress-sense. He always puts a twist on his sharp tailoring by tucking his trousers into his boots and casually rolling up the sleeves on his fitted blazer.

JAY

Indie-kid Jay has a laid-back sense of style which matches his personality. He loves low-key grunge, which always looks street-wise and savvy especially when off-set by his cute, boy-next-door face and curly floppy hair.

THE FAME GAME

Grab your friends and have a giggle acting out some The Wanted songs.

How to play

1 Write all of the song titles on scraps of paper. Fold them up and put them in a bowl.

2 Take turns picking a piece of paper out of the bowl.

3 Without speaking, help your friends try to guess what the title is.

4 Make it trickier by timing yourselves – three minutes each!

5 The person who guesses the most titles correctly wins!

Here are some to get you started:

Hi & Low

All Time Low

Heart Vacancy

Replace Your Heart

Say It On The Radio

Lose My Mind

Let's Get Ugly

Weakness

Behind Bars

Personal Soldier

Golden

The Way I Feel

A Good Day For Love To Die

Glad You Came

Gold Forever

Made

35

SCRAMBLED LYRICS

Can you recognize this lot of mixed-up lyrics?

1 Who od oyu pu omrf na lal mite wlo

2 Os setl og mwoseehre on neo sele nca ese

3 Sest tge gylu

4 Mi ngona selo ym dmni

5 Uoy wonk I venre twna ot trhu uyo

6 Hse si ym kwesesan

7 Nda ew vlie treaonh yda

8 Wno a hpwsirse glalcin em

THE WANTED FANS

DID YOU KNOW?

Tom has smelly feet!

Max would love to go on a date to a lizard house!

Nathan used to have to get up at 5am to make the three-hour trip from Gloucester to London to go to stage school!

Tom has a scar on his nose from chicken pox.

Tom hates not being able to get back to all the fans who've tweeted him.

Nathan would most hate to do a cover of The Birdy Song.

Jay has a phobia of polystyrene.

Siva and Jay both have twin brothers.

Siva loves getting Skittles from fans.

TUNE IN

Favourite bands

The Wanted's sound is a unique urban blend of poppy tunes and edgy beats with some super cool indie riffs thrown in. It's no wonder it's so diverse when you look at the very different mix of bands the boys have all been influenced by!

Tom	Oasis, Stereophonics
Max	Queen, Oasis
Jay	Coldplay, Damien Rice, Cat Stevens
Siva	John Legend
Nathan	Boyz II Men

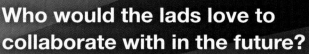

Who would the lads love to collaborate with in the future?

Dizzee Rascal

Florence and the Machine

Justin Bieber. According to Siva, the guys have totally caught Bieber fever!

JLS

The boys are huge fans of JLS and will be forever grateful to them for blazing the boy band trail.

"If they hadn't brought the whole boy band thing back I don't know if we could actually have done it," smiles Jay. "As opposed to taking them on, because we would fail we will try and leech on to their success and get dragged up by them."
"We're not trying to copy them," says Tom. "We want to be ourselves."

SAY WHAT?

"I slap on the moisturizer and sleep on silk sheets so I don't get wrinkles."
Siva

"As long as we don't get called 'man band' that sounds a bit strange."
Max

"I'm a bit of an old man really."
Nathan

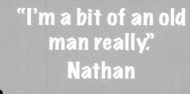

"I think this is a bit better than joining the circus."
Jay

WORDSEARCH

```
S Z G V G M A X S S E A Q D A
V O S D L L G J C L W G T A L
G Z F B B V A B P L A F P D L
S X E X I K R D K W W C J I T
I Z R R V I S M Y C B I O V I
G E F F E N R E C O R D S V M
T N R R A O D S Y D U S F W E
A O S F A J P B F Z L C S C L
V X M E J Z A U B E E Q A U O
I P K W M N M B G N C K V M W
S J G E D N A H T A N C X O E
L T W H R E M A A R L Z A Q D
H E C C S J L Q M W M Z J N E
S E Q R S W M T E U C D A R T
G M Y Y Y H P F Q S R Y Y R F
```

Can you find these hidden words?

GLADYOUCAME   BOYBAND

ALLTIMELOW

FANS

MAX   GEFFENRECORDS

NATHAN   TOM   JAY

SIVA

VOCALS

Answers on Page 60.

CELEBRITY CHAIN

Solve the clues to find the links between Nathan and this fierce singer

1. Nathan Sykes went to the same school as Spice Girl xxxx xxxxxx (4, 6)
2. Who sang in the same band as xxxx xxxxxxxxx (4, 9)
3. Who once dated xxxxxx, xxxxxxxx (,6 8)
4. Who is band mates with xxxx xxxxxx (4, 6)
5. Who is a fellow judge on the X Factor with xxxxx xxxxxxx (5, 7)
6. Who was in Destiny's Child with xxxxxx xxxxxxx (6,7)

Answers on Page 60.

SPOT THE DIFFERENCE

Take a close look at these two photos, can you spot the 7 differences between them?

Answers on Page 60.

A–Z

A is for All Time Low - their amazing, unforgettable debut single!

B is for Bananakick - Jay's nickname at school because he couldn't kick a football in a straight line.

C is for carrot leg jeans. Max loves them.

D is for Domino's Pizza. Max's all-time favourite.

E is for Eurovision. Nathan came third in the Junior Eurovision Song Contest.

F is for fans. The boys really love theirs.

G is for Geffen Records.

H is for Heart Vacancy.

I is for Indian and Italian - Tom's favourite foods.

J is for Jay.

K is for Kate Thornton - Nathan's dream woman!

L is for lizards.

M is for Max.

is for Nathan.

 is for Oasis. Tom's favourite band.

 is for Preston North End FC who Max used to play for.

 is for quintuple.

 is for Rhianna. She texted Siva.

 is for Siva.

 is for Tom.

 is for the boys' urban style.

 is for Vests - part of the Wanted uniform.

 is for Wanted Mania.

 is for X Factor where we first saw Max.

 is for Youngest. Nathan is the baby of the group.

Z is for Zen - Siva's role in the group.

LIVE YOUR LIFE
THE WANTED WAY

Get a little bit of Jay, Nathan, Siva, Max and Tom in your world every single day!

1. Get some scented candles for your room, zen Siva loves them.

2. Whack on some Queen and throw some crazy shapes a la Max.

3. Tuck into some Italian food – Tom can't get enough of it.

4. Learn how to play the bagpipes like Nathan.

5. Go for a kick-about in your local park and make Max proud.

6. Tidy your bedroom like Nathan...

7. ... And then mess it up like the rest of the boys.

8. Rock earrings like Tom.

9. Make like Max and wear some carrot leg jeans

10. Change your Facebook pic to one of the boys to show your Wanted love.

THE FUTURE

Right now, the boys are riding high and their star shows no sign of falling. They've made the kind of start that other boy bands could only dream of, but they know they have to keep on proving themselves and are working their stylish socks off.

"We have to keep putting the hours in," says Jay. "And hope people like what we do."

For a manufactured boy band, The Wanted have broken out of any mould that could have cramped or altered them and have become an even bigger sensation because of it.

They may be super stars but the boys are still keeping their feet firmly on the ground. At heart they will always be ordinary lads from normal backgrounds and will never forget where they came from or the fans who helped get them there. They have such a groundswell of support, which is growing all the time, that it would be impossible for them to disappear from the scene overnight.

"You can succeed with whatever you're happy with," Siva

Knowing the lads, they're going to be entertaining us with their unique mix of urban pop for a long long time to come. They're having the time of their lives. And we wouldn't have it any other way.

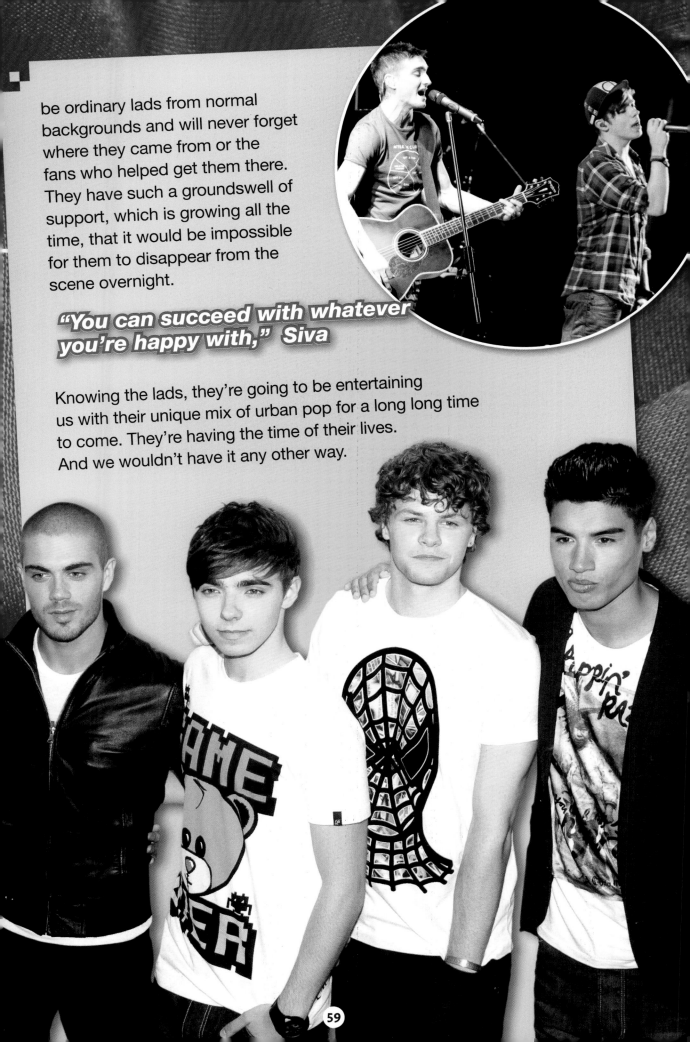

ANSWERS

Are You The Biggest Wanted Fan? (p26)

1 (b) Nathan
2 (c) Jay
3 (b) Max
4 (c) Max
5 (a) Scorpio
6 (c) Sitting on the Dock of the Bay by Otis Redding
7 (b) Nathan
8 (c) The Good, the bad and the Ugly
9 (a) Model
10 (a) Tom

Scrambled Lyrics (p38)

1. How do you get up from an all-time low?
2. So let's go somewhere else no one else can see
3. Let's get ugly
4. I'm gonna lose my mind
5. You know I never want to hurt you
6. She is my weakness
7. And we live another day
8. Now a whispers calling me

Wordsearch (p46)

S	Z	G	V	G	M	A	X	S	S	E	A	Q	D	A
V	O	S	D	L	L	G	J	C	L	W	G	T	A	L
G	Z	F	B	B	V	A	B	P	L	A	F	P	D	L
S	X	E	X	I	K	R	D	K	W	W	C	J	I	T
I	Z	R	R	V	I	S	M	Y	C	B	I	O	V	I
G	E	F	F	E	N	R	E	C	O	R	D	S	V	M
T	N	R	R	A	O	D	S	Y	D	U	S	F	W	E
A	O	S	F	A	J	P	B	F	Z	L	C	S	C	L
V	X	M	E	J	Z	A	U	B	E	E	Q	A	U	O
I	P	K	W	M	N	M	B	G	N	C	K	V	M	W
S	J	G	E	D	N	A	H	T	A	N	C	X	O	E
L	T	W	H	R	E	M	A	A	R	L	Z	A	Q	D
H	E	C	C	S	J	L	Q	M	W	M	Z	J	N	E
S	E	Q	R	S	W	M	T	E	U	C	D	A	R	T
G	M	Y	Y	Y	H	P	F	Q	S	R	Y	Y	R	F

Celebrity Chain (p48)

1. Emma Bunton
2. Geri Halliwell
3. Robbie Williams
4. Gary Barlow
5. Kelly Rowland
6. Beyonce Knowles

Spot the Difference (p49)

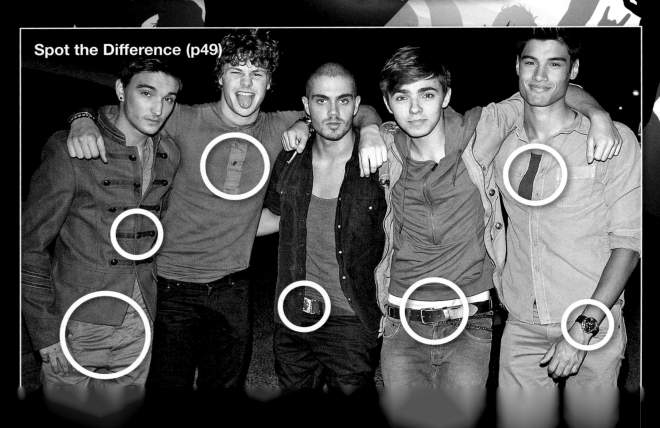

WHERE'S *THE WANTED*?